Welcome

to the Daily 5 Workshop. We've prepared this collection of forms, quotes, and questions to help you apply what you've learned when you return to the classroom.

The text you hold has reflection questions sprinkled throughout the pages—more than a workbook, this is a "thinkbook" designed to help you pause and reflect on the learning from today's presentation. Since you can't talk back to us in the midst of presenting, these reflection questions should help you "talk back" to the ideas from the workshop, wrestling with how to make them your own.

We're hoping this resource helps you in that journey of integrating the learning from this workshop into your classroom. We are so honored you are finding a place for our work in your teaching. Happy reading, happy thinking, and happy learning!

Gail & Joan

Educational Design, LLC, 1911 SW Campus Drive #683, Federal Way, WA 98023
www.thedailycafe.com

Library of Congress Cataloging in Publication Data Pending

ISBN 978-1-61892-000-3

Cover and interior design by Madeline Boushey

Manufactured in the United States of America

View handouts online:
http://www.thedailycafe.com/articles/handouts-daily-5

Handouts

Feedback Survey

Contents

About our Websites	i
Agenda	ii
Our Learning Line	1
How Much Do Student's Read?	3
Read to Self	6
Three Ways to Read a Book	7
I PICK "Good-Fit Books"	8
Work on Writing	9
Read to Someone	10
Preteach Read to Someone Behaviors	11
Listen to Reading	12
Word Work	13
Structure of Daily 5 and CAFE	14-16
Differentiating Daily 5 and CAFE	17-18
10 Steps to Teaching and Learning Independence	20
Daily 5 Tasks	21
Must-Have Student Behaviors	22
Stamina Chart	23
Levels of Support for Barometer Children	27
Minutes of Stamina Before We Introduce the Next Daily 5	29
Launching Daily 5	30-32
Keeping Track of Daily 5 Choices	33
Daily 5 Check-In Form	34
Our Learning Line (with Trust & Respect)	36
Literacy Block Schedule Samples	38-39
Guest Teacher Plans	43-44
Parent Letter Introducing Daily 5	45
Gathering Space and Focus Lessons	46
Bibliography	47-48
Certificate of Completion	49
Graduate Credit Information	50-54

The Daily Cafe is an online resource, which is updated weekly to energize your literacy instruction. It provides professional development support to those in all stages of the Daily 5, The CAFE System, Math Daily 3, Classroom Design, and everything in between. The Daily CAFE is the only place to learn the latest research and teachings of The 2 Sisters.

www.thedailycafe.com

The CCPensieve (short for CAFE Conferring Pensieve) is a web-based conferring notebook, which goes beyond the capabilities of pen and paper at a comparable price to setting up a paper-conferring notebook. It allows teachers to share student progress data with each other, parents, or other essential educators who have an interest in the progress of their students.

www.ccpensieve.com

Features

- Hundreds of professional video segments—taped by award-winning videographers in K–6 classrooms, you'll see everything from Word Work to check-in procedures to individual conferences with students of widely varying abilities.

- Templates for strategy groups, conferring, and whole class management and assessment.

- Design tools for creating a warm, inviting, and smart literacy environment.

- Detailed descriptions of the "nitty gritty" processes for everything from organizing assessments to troubleshooting with students who struggle to stay on task.

- Guidance on how to integrate assessment with the ongoing work of reading and writing instruction.

- Portraits of veteran and novice teachers trying out new strategies in their classroom, and receiving coaching from The 2 Sisters as they do.

- Literacy tips delivered weekly to your inbox.

- Discussion board to share literacy instructional ideas with other teachers.

Features

- Real-Time student sharing between users

- Printer friendly PDF and CSV reports

- Individual and group conferring with the following subjects: reading, writing, word work, science, social studies, and other/custom.

- Individual CAFE Menu for each student

- Self populating keeping track sheet

- Calendar to schedule meetings

- Reading level data sheet

- Interactive CAFE Menus with links to TheDailyCAFE.com for professional development

- Student archiving

- Secure account for use with any device

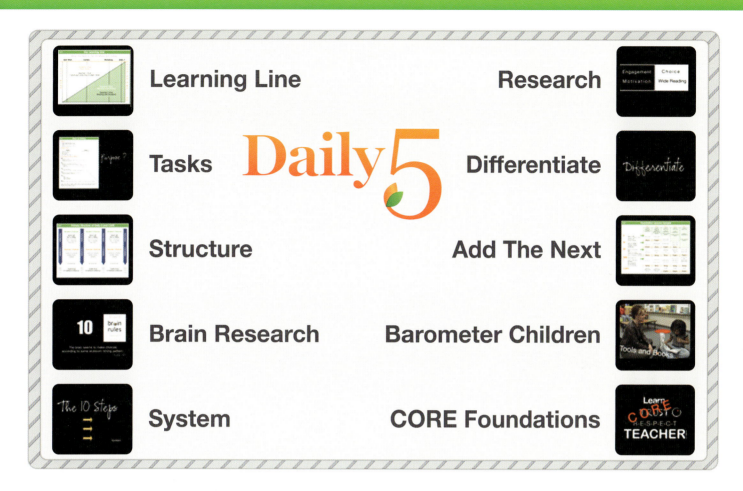

Learning Line

Tasks

Daily 5

Structure

Brain Research

System

Research

Differentiate

Add The Next

Barometer Children

CORE Foundations

Take your learning beyond the pages of this book

QR Codes

QR codes will take you to videos and further reading to expand and enrich your learning. Try scanning this one!

Think Bubble

Look for pages with this think bubble, to reflect on how your new learning relates to your current teaching.

Further Reading

Look for pages with this book in the corner, for selected readings and samples relevent to the presentation.

Our Learning Line

What the Rest of the Students Are Doing

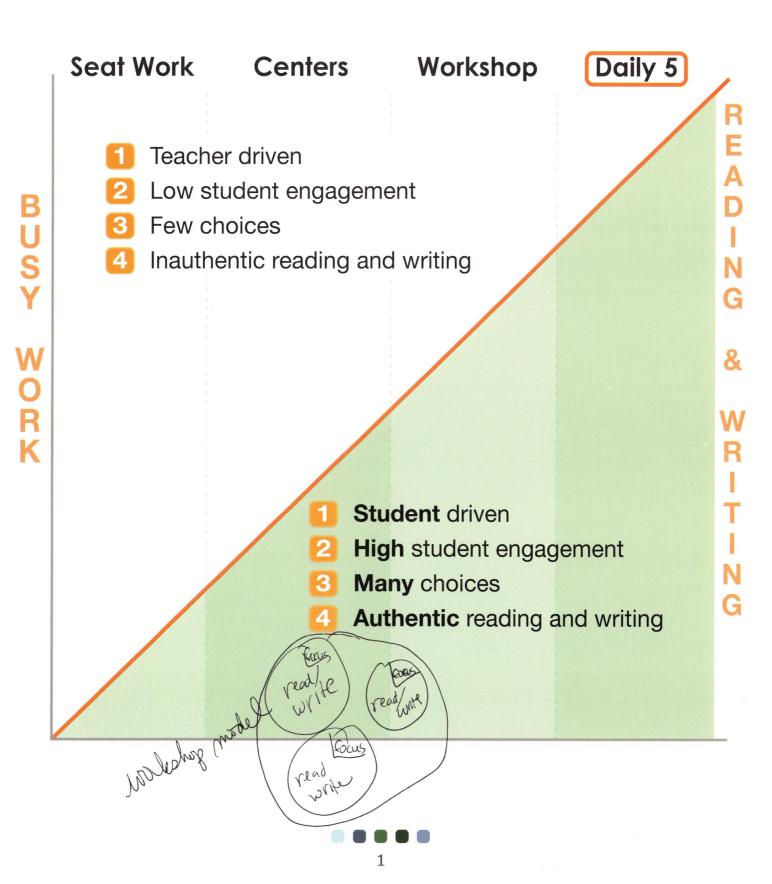

Seat Work **Centers** **Workshop** Daily 5

BUSY WORK

READING & WRITING

1. Teacher driven
2. Low student engagement
3. Few choices
4. Inauthentic reading and writing

1. **Student** driven
2. **High** student engagement
3. **Many** choices
4. **Authentic** reading and writing

workshop model
focus read/write
focus read/write
focus read write

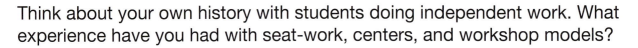
Think about your own history with students doing independent work. What experience have you had with seat-work, centers, and workshop models?

Why did you make the change to Daily 5 for independent work? (If you haven't made the change yet, why are you considering a change?)

What successful elements of seat-work, centers, or a workshop model do you hope to continue with a Daily 5 structure?

How Much Do Students Read?

Middle-Class Fifth Graders
(Anderson, Wilson, and Fielding, 1988)

Plus 10 Minutes per Day...
(Adams, 2006)

Percentile	Minutes per Day	Words per Year	Minutes per Day	Words per Year	Percent Increase in Word Exposure
98	65.0	4,358,000	75.0	5,028,462	15%
90	21.1	1,823,000	31.1	2,686,981	47%
80	14.2	1,146,000	24.2	1,953,042	70%
70	9.6	622,000	19.6	1,269,917	104%
60	6.5	432,000	16.5	1,096,615	154%
50	4.6	282,000	14.6	895,043	217%
40	3.2	200,000	13.2	825,000	313%
30	1.8	106,000	11.8	694,889	556%
20	0.7	21,000	10.7	321,000	1,429%
10	0.1	8,000	10.1	*Low minutes read values, make statistical inference invalid and unreliable.*	
2	0.0	0	10.0		

Based on reading level, ~300,000 words

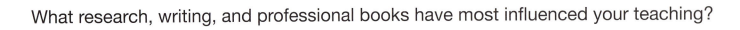

What research, writing, and professional books have most influenced your teaching?

What connections do you make between Daily 5 and your favorite research and professional writing?

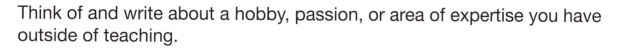

Think of and write about a hobby, passion, or area of expertise you have outside of teaching.

How did you acquire the skills necessary to reach expert status?

What connections do you make to literacy instruction?

Foundation Lesson

Teach this lesson before launching Read to Self:
- Three Ways to Read a Book

Launch

Use the 10 Steps to Independence to launch Read to Self.

Step 1. Identify what is to be taught: Read to Self.

Step 2. Set a purpose and create a sense of urgency for Read to Self:
- It is the best way to become better readers.
- It is fun.

Step 3. Record desirable behaviors of Read to Self on an I-chart.
- Sample I-Chart:

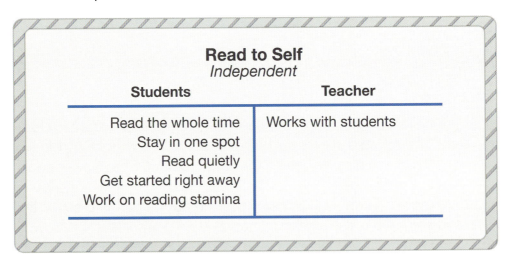

Read to Self	
Independent	
Students	**Teacher**
Read the whole time	Works with students
Stay in one spot	
Read quietly	
Get started right away	
Work on reading stamina	

Step 4. Model most-desirable behaviors.

Step 5. Model least-desirable behaviors, then most-desirable behaviors again.

Step 6. Place students around the room.

Step 7. Practice and build stamina.

Step 8. Stay out of the way.

Step 9. Use a quiet signal to bring students back to the gathering place

Step 10. Conduct a group check-in; ask, "How did it go?"

Foundation Lessons

Teach the following as focus lessons during the launch of Read to Self:
- Three Ways to Read a Book
  (reteach during launch in addition to before launch)
- Choose a Successful Spot
- I PICK a Good-Fit Book

Three Ways to Read a Book

We find this to be a foundational lesson before we introduce Read to Self. Its necessity became very clear one year as we were asking students to read to themselves and about half of our first graders chimed in, "I don't know how to read." How could we possibly ask students to read independently if they truly did not possess reading skills?

At that time we would partner students up or create a center for them to do, because they couldn't read words yet. We heard a similar response when asking our older students who were ELL, just arriving to our country and not able to read English. Without books in the 30+ different languages in our schools we felt puzzled and frustrated. To us it was a bit like "the chicken or the egg."

As we researched beginning reading acquisition, we discovered that children learn to read by engaging in the act of reading by "Reading the Pictures," "Reading the Words," and "Retelling a Familiar Story."

With this in mind we begin our teaching each year with modeling "Three Ways to Read" using a short picture book. It sounds like this . . .

"Girls and boys, there are three ways to read, and I am going to show you how to do all three. First I am going to **read the pictures**. Let's see, the cover of this book has a big world and five different people on the front; I think this book is going to be about these five people. Here is the first page. Here are those five people again, and there are white houses in the background. They are holding a sign." We continue through the story, telling about the pictures. At the end of the reading we say, "Boys and girls, I just showed you one way to read and that is by reading the pictures. I am going to write that down on our chart to remind us of the three ways to read.

"Now I am going to show you another way to read. I am going to **read the words**." We then read the same book, but this time we read the words. At the end of the story, we remind the students that reading the words is another way to read and we add "Read the Words" to our chart of ways to read.

We then tell the students there is another way to read and that is to **retell a familiar story**. We use the same book and retell the story by looking at the pictures and saying what is happening.

The first time we did this, we didn't have anyone say, "I cannot silent read, because I don't know how to read." From this day forward, all students were able to be engaged in reading by reading the pictures, reading the words, or retelling a story. We even teach this lesson to older students. We want to remind our older students that reading pictures is a critical strategy, especially if we are reading nonfiction, graphic novels, and some textbooks. So with our older students we model reading the pictures with one of these genres.

I look at a book

P urpose

I nterest

C omprehend

K now all the words

10 Steps to Independence
Work on Writing

Foundation Lessons

Teach these lessons before launching Work on Writing:

- Underline Words You Don't Know How to Spell, and Move On
- Set Up a Notebook
- Choose What to Write About

Launch

Use the 10 Steps to Independence to launch Work on Writing.

Step 1. Identify what is to be taught: Work on Writing.

Step 2. Set a purpose and create a sense of urgency for Work on Writing:

- It helps us become better writers.
- It helps us become better readers.
- It increases fluency of writing.
- It is fun.

Step 3. Record desirable behaviors of Work on Writing on an I-chart. Sample I-Chart:

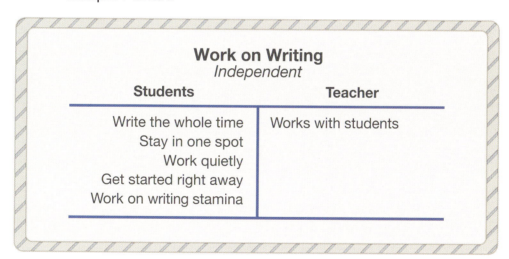

Work on Writing *Independent*	
Students	**Teacher**
Write the whole time Stay in one spot Work quietly Get started right away Work on writing stamina	Works with students

Step 4. Model most-desirable behaviors.

Step 5. Model least-desirable behaviors, then most-desirable behaviors again.

Step 6. Place students around the room.

Step 7. Practice and build stamina.

Step 8. Stay out of the way.

Step 9. Use a quiet signal to bring students back to the gathering place

Step 10. Conduct a group check-in; ask, "How did it go?"

Foundation Lessons

Teach this lesson before launching Read to Someone:

- EEKK (elbow, elbow, knee, knee)
- Voice Level
- Check for Understanding
- How Partners Read
- How to Get Started
- Coaching or Time?
- How to Choose a Partner

Launch

Use the 10 Steps to Independence to launch Read to Someone.

Step 1. Identify what is to be taught: Read to Someone.

Step 2. Set a purpose and create a sense of urgency for Read to Someone:

- It helps us improve our fluency.
- It helps us practice Check for Understanding and Comprehension.
- It is fun.

Step 3. Record desirable behaviors of Read to Someone on an I-chart.

- Sample I-Chart:

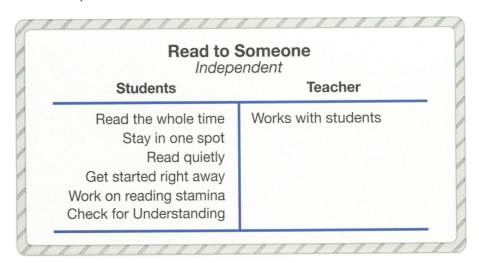

Read to Someone
Independent

Students	Teacher
Read the whole time Stay in one spot Read quietly Get started right away Work on reading stamina Check for Understanding	Works with students

Step 4. Model most-desirable behaviors.

Step 5. Model least-desirable behaviors, then most-desirable behaviors again.

Step 6. Place students around the room.

Step 7. Practice and build stamina.

Step 8. Stay out of the way.

Step 9. Use a quiet signal to bring students back to the gathering place

Step 10. Conduct a group check-in; ask, "How did it go?"

Preteach Read to Someone Behaviors—Plan Ahead

- Book Choice
- Picking Partners
- How to Sit
- Order of Reading
- Listening
- Talking About Book
- Coaching or Time
- Not for Everyone
- Limit the Number

10 Steps to Independence
Listen to Reading

Foundation Lessons

Teach these lessons before launching Listen to Reading:
- Set Up the Technology
- Listen and Follow Along
- Manage Fairness and Equitable Use with a Limited Number of Devices

Launch

Use the 10 Steps to Independence to launch Listen to Reading.

Step 1. Identify what is to be taught: Listen to Reading.

Step 2. Set a purpose and create a sense of urgency for Listen to Reading:
- It helps us become better readers.
- It helps us learn and understand new words.
- It is fun.

Step 3. Record desirable behaviors of Listen to Reading on an I-chart.
- Sample I-Chart:

Listen to Reading *Independent*	
Students	**Teacher**
Get materials out	Works with students
Listen the whole time	
May listen to another story if time	
Follow along using pictures and/or words	
Stay in one spot	
Listen quietly	
Get started quickly	
Put materials away neatly	

Step 4. Model most-desirable behaviors.

Step 5. Model least-desirable behaviors, then most-desirable behaviors again.

Step 6. Place students around the room.

Step 7. Practice and build stamina.

Step 8. Stay out of the way.

Step 9. Use a quiet signal to bring students back to the gathering place.

Step 10. Conduct a group check-in; ask, "How did it go?"

Foundation Lessons

Teach this lesson before launching Word Work:
- Set Up and Clean Up Materials
- Choose Materials and Words to Use
- Choose a Successful Spot

Optional Materials

Individual whiteboards
White board table
Magnet letters
Beans
Letter stamps
Colored markers
Clay

Launch

Use the 10 Steps to Independence to launch Word Work.

Step 1. Identify what is to be taught: Word Work.

Step 2. Set a purpose and create a sense of urgency for Word Work:
- It helps us improve our fluency.
- It helps us practice Check for Understanding and Comprehension.
- It is fun.

Step 3. Record desirable behaviors of Word Work on an I-chart. (see samples below)

Step 4. Model most-desirable behaviors.

Step 5. Model least-desirable behaviors, then most-desirable behaviors again.

Step 6. Place students around the room.

Step 7. Practice and build stamina.

Step 8. Stay out of the way.

Step 9. Use a quiet signal to bring students back to the gathering place

Step 10. Conduct a group check-in; ask, "How did it go?"

Sample I-Charts:

Set Up Materials
Independent

Students	Teacher
Get materials out	Works with students
Choose a locations where you and others can be successful	
Set up quietly	
Stay in one spot	
Get started quickly	

How to Use Materials
Independent

Students	Teacher
Work the whole time	Works with students
Stay in one spot except to get and return materials	
May return one set of materials and get another set to work with before round is over	
Work quietly	
Work on stamina	
Try your best	

Clean Up Materials
Independent

Students	Teacher
Everyone using materials helps put them away	Works with students
Materials go back in their original container	
Return materials to the same spot	
Leave materials neat	
Clean quietly	
Get started cleaning right away	
Clean quickly	

Focus Lesson — 7–10 minutes

Student Choices
Read to Self
Work on Writing
Read to Someone
Listen to Reading
Word Work

Teacher Choices
Individual Conferring
Guided Groups
Assessing

15 Minutes

Focus Lesson — 7–10 minutes

Student Choices
Read to Self
Work on Writing
Read to Someone
Listen to Reading
Word Work

Teacher Choices
Individual Conferring
Guided Groups
Assessing

15 Minutes

Focus Lesson — 7–10 minutes

Student Choices
Read to Self
Work on Writing
Read to Someone
Listen to Reading
Word Work

Teacher Choices
Individual Conferring
Guided Groups
Assessing

15 Minutes

Focus Lesson — 7–10 minutes

Student Choices
Read to Self
Work on Writing
Read to Someone
Listen to Reading
Word Work

Teacher Choices
Individual Conferring
Guided Groups
Assessing

15 Minutes

Focus Lesson — 7–10 minutes

Student Choices
Read to Self
Work on Writing
Read to Someone
Listen to Reading
Word Work

Teacher Choices
Individual Conferring
Guided Groups
Assessing

15 Minutes

Focus Lesson — 7–10 minutes

Structure of Daily 5 and CAFE

Focus Lesson	Student Choices	Focus Lesson	Student Choices	Focus Lesson	Student Choices	Focus Lesson

Focus Lesson · 7–10 minutes

Student Choices

Read to Self
Work on Writing
Read to Someone
Listen to Reading
Word Work

Teacher Choices

Individual Conferring
Guided Groups
Assessing

15 Minutes

20–30 Minutes

Focus Lesson · 7–10 minutes

Student Choices

Read to Self
Work on Writing
Read to Someone
Listen to Reading
Word Work

Teacher Choices

Individual Conferring
Guided Groups
Assessing

15 Minutes

20–30 Minutes

Focus Lesson · 7–10 minutes

Student Choices

Read to Self
Work on Writing
Read to Someone
Listen to Reading
Word Work

Teacher Choices

Individual Conferring
Guided Groups
Assessing

15 Minutes

20–30 Minutes

Focus Lesson · 7–10 minutes

---

1 Guided Group
and
3–4 Individual Conferences

1 Guided Group
and
3–4 Individual Conferences

1 Guided Group
and
3–4 Individual Conferences

Structure of Daily 5 and CAFE

Focus Lesson — 7–10 minutes

Student Choices

Read to Self
Work on Writing
Read to Someone
Listen to Reading
Word Work

Teacher Choices

Individual Conferring
Guided Groups
Assessing

30–40 Minutes

1–2 Groups
and
3–6 Individual Conferences

Focus Lesson — 7–10 minutes

Student Choices

Read to Self
Work on Writing
Read to Someone
Listen to Reading
Word Work

Teacher Choices

Individual Conferring
Guided Groups
Assessing

30–40 Minutes

1–2 Groups
and
3–6 Individual Conferences

Focus Lesson — 7–10 minutes

Reading

Differentiate

all student {
Read to Self
Read to Someone
Listen to Reading
} Choose 1

Writing

all Work on Writing

Word Work

behavior issues stop watch then go

10 minutes only

Must do read + write everyday

Differentiating Daily 5 and CAFE

This chart addresses some of the differences between grade levels implementing Daily 5 and CAFE.

Keep in mind that **changes are made** based on **professional judgment** of each teacher and the varying **needs of their students**.

	Kindergarten	Beginning	Advanced
Number of Daily 5 Rounds	2-3	3	2
Average Minutes Per Round	15-20	20-30	30-40
Must Do Each Day	Read to Self Work on Writing	Read to Self Work on Writing	Read to Self Work on Writing
Focus Lessons Duration	5-7 minutes	5-8 minutes	5-11 minutes
Focus Lesson Content	Comprehension Accuracy Expand Vocabulary	Comprehension Accuracy Fluency Expand Vocabulary	Comprehension Expand Vocabulary
Small Group Lesson Content *(as needed)*	Comprehension Accuracy Fluency Expand Vocabulary	Comprehension Accuracy Fluency Expand Vocabulary	Comprehension Accuracy Fluency Expand Vocabulary
Small Group	if needed	if needed	if needed
One-on-One Content	Comprehension Accuracy Fluency Expand Vocabulary	Comprehension Accuracy Fluency Expand Vocabulary	Comprehension Accuracy Fluency Expand Vocabulary
One-on-One Conference	9-12 students each day	9-12 students each day	9-12 students each day
Interactive Read Aloud Lesson Content *(Read at a different time of the day)*	Fluency Expand Vocabulary	Fluency Expand Vocabulary	Fluency Expand Vocabulary
Writing Workshop	Integrated into Daily 5 Or can be separate depending on time	Separate time Students still write during Daily 5 for the fluency of writing	Integrated into Daily 5

Based on the brain research from Dr. Ken Wesson, the age of the child indicates the number of minutes they can maintain stamina in whole-class and small-group lessons. In other words, eight-year-olds can sustain eight minutes of instruction, and eleven-year-olds can attend to eleven minutes of direct teaching.

Take a minute to reflect on your teaching or lesson plans from the last week. Do the length of your whole-class and small-group lessons match the age of your students?

What ideas for brain and body breaks from the Daily 5 workshop might you integrate into your classroom routines to shorten your lessons?

What structural changes might be necessary in your literacy program to chunk instruction into shorter segments?

10 Steps to Teaching and Learning Independence

Chunk 1

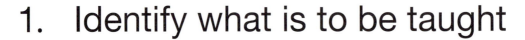

1. Identify what is to be taught

2. Setting a purpose—create a sense of urgency

3. Record desired behaviors on I-chart
   (Start with 2 behaviors)

Chunk 2

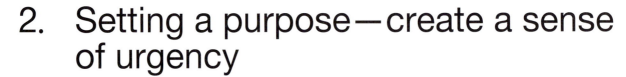

4. Model most-desirable behaviors

5. Model least-desirable behaviors, then desirable

Chunk 3

6. Place students around the room

7. Practice and build stamina

8. Stay out of the way

9. Quiet signal—come back to group

10. Group check-in—"How did it go?"

Daily 5 Tasks

Creating a Sense of Urgency

- **Read to Self**
The best way to become a better reader is to practice each day with "Good-fit" books that you have selected yourself, and it is fun!

- **Work on Writing**
As with reading, the best way to become a better writer is to write each day, and it is fun!

- **Read to Someone**
Partner reading provides opportunities to practice strategies, improve fluency, check for understanding, and hear your own voice while sharing in the learning community, and it is fun!

- **Word Work**
Expanded vocabulary leads to greater fluency in reading, therefore increasing comprehension. Becoming more proficient as a speller leads to writing fluency and the ability to get your ideas down on paper, and it is fun!

- **Listen to Reading**
Just hearing fluent and expressive reading of good literature expands your vocabulary, helps build your stamina, and will make you a better reader, and it is fun!

Read the whole time

Stay in one spot

Read quietly

Start right away

Work on reading stamina

Stamina Chart

25											
24											
23											
22											
21											
20											
19											
18											
17											
16											
15											
14											
13											
12											
11											
10											
9											
8											
7											
6											
5											
4											
3											
2											
1											

minutes   **date**

S T A M I N A

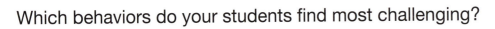

Which behaviors do your students find most challenging?

What ideas from the Daily 5 presentation might you try in your classroom to help students with these behaviors?

What other changes to your I-charts are you considering based on what you've learned in the Daily 5 presentation?

We used to check in with... *thumbs up, thumbs down, thumbs to the side.*

But now we check in with...

1 Below Standard
2 Approaching Standard
3 Meeting Standard
4 Exceeding Standard

(thanks to Carlene Bickford of Waterville, Maine)

How do your students check in?

How do you use the information from check in to revise your teaching plans?

How might you integrate more goal setting into your check in precedures?

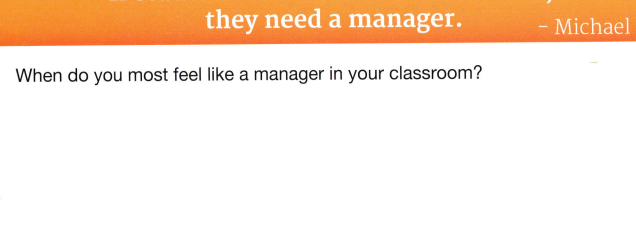

**If students can't do the task, they need a teacher.
If students can do the task but don't,
they need a manager.** – Michael Grinder

When do you most feel like a manager in your classroom?

When do you most feel like a teacher?

How has Daily 5 shifted the balance between management and teaching in your classroom?

Levels of Support for Barometer Children

● **Level 1: *Reflection***
The teacher reflects on their own teaching practice, asking these questions:
1. Did I teach the 10 Steps to Independence explicitly?
2. Am I visually keeping my eyes and body away from the barometer child?
3. Do I continually use a respectful voice level and tone (no sharp tongue)?
4. Remember that deposits must be made before withdrawal.
5. Chart teacher deposits.
6. Green card.

On back of lanyard - when color always - child knows doing a good job

Tracking Positive Behaviors

9–10	10–11	11–12	12–1	1–2	2–3

● **Level 2: *Extra Support***
1. Student stays in during recess for 2–3 minutes practicing most-desirable behavior.
2. Student continues to practice during recess for 3–5 days until behavior starts to change. If independent behavior is not improving, move to Level 3.

● **Level 3: *In-Class Modifications***
1. Square yard of fabric, two sand timers, book box, small bag of manipulatives (ex: Legos, play dough, different reading materials). Teach student to work with body on fabric, using the sand timer, alternating between reading and manipulation of tools.

● **Level 4: *Gradual Release of In-Class Modifications***
1. Barometer Student Sandwich—When conferring, check on barometer child first, then move to a different student, return to barometer child for a quick check-in, move to another student, then repeat. Sandwich support for our barometer children between our support for other children.

● **Level 5: Whole-School Support**
1. Photos of Barometer Children—Introduce them to the staff.
2. Walk About—Students run errands for the class, with a purposeful intent.

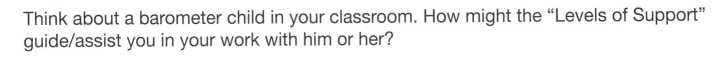

Think about a barometer child in your classroom. How might the "Levels of Support" guide/assist you in your work with him or her?

What unique challenges does this child present?

What in-class modifications might you try?

Which colleagues might help you by observing and discussing the child with you? Why did you choose them?

Kindergarten = 7–8 minutes

Primary = 10–12 minutes

Intermediate = 12–14 minutes

Foundation Lessons

	Day 1	Day 2	Day 3	Day 4	Day 5
R Read to Self 3 Ways to Read a Book Where to Sit Good-Fit Books 	Launch Read to Self 10 Steps to Independence	Launch Read to Self 10 Steps to Independence Review and Build Stamina	Launch Read to Self 10 Steps to Independence Review and Build Stamina	Launch Read to Self 10 Steps to Independence Review and Build Stamina	Launch Read to Self 10 Steps to Independence Review and Build Stamina
W Work on Writing Ideas for Writing Underline Words Notebooks					
RS Read to Someone EEKK I Read, You Read Check for Understanding How to Choose a Partner					
WW Word Work **L Listen to Reading** Materials What Materials Setup/Cleanup Use of Materials					
CAFE Goals/Strategies					

Launching Daily 5 Sample

Foundation Lessons

	Day 1	Day 2	Day 3	Day 4	Day 5
R — **Read to Self** 3 Ways to Read a Book Where to Sit Good-Fit Books	Launch Read to Self 10 Steps to Independence Good-Fit Books **Movement**	Launch Read to Self 10 Steps to Independence Review and Build Stamina 3 Ways to Read Good-Fit Books **Poem**	Launch Read to Sel 10 Steps to Independence Review and Build Stamina 3 Ways to Read Good-Fit Books	Launch Read to Self 10 Steps to Independence Review and Build Stamina 3 Ways to Read Good-Fit Books Underline Words	Launch Read to Self 10 Steps to Independence Review and Build Stamina
W — **Work on Writing** Ideas for Writing Underline Words Notebooks	Underline Words **Poem**	Underline Words Set Up Notebook **Movement**	Underline Words Ideas for Writing **Poem**	**Movement**	
RS — **Read to Someone** EEKK I Read, You Read Check for Understanding How to Choose a Partner	Check for Understanding **Movement**	Check for Understanding EEKK **Song**	Check for Understanding EEKK I Read, You Read **Movement**	Ideas for Writing Check for Understanding EEKK **Poem**	3 Ways to Read Good-Fit Books Underline Words **Poem**
WW — **Word Work** **Listen to Reading** Materials What Materials Setup/Cleanup Use of Materials	Material Setup **Picture Book**	Material Setup Material Cleanup **Picture Book**	Material Setup Material Cleanup Using Materials **Picture Book**	I Read, You Read Material Setup Material Cleanup Using Materials **Picture Book**	Ideas for Writing EEKK I Read, You Read Material Setup Material Cleanup **Picture Book**
CAFE **Goals/Strategies**	Check for Understanding Getting to Know the CAFE	Check for Understanding Getting to Know the CAFE	Strategy **Poem**	Strategy **Poem**	Strategy **Poem**

31

Launching Daily 5

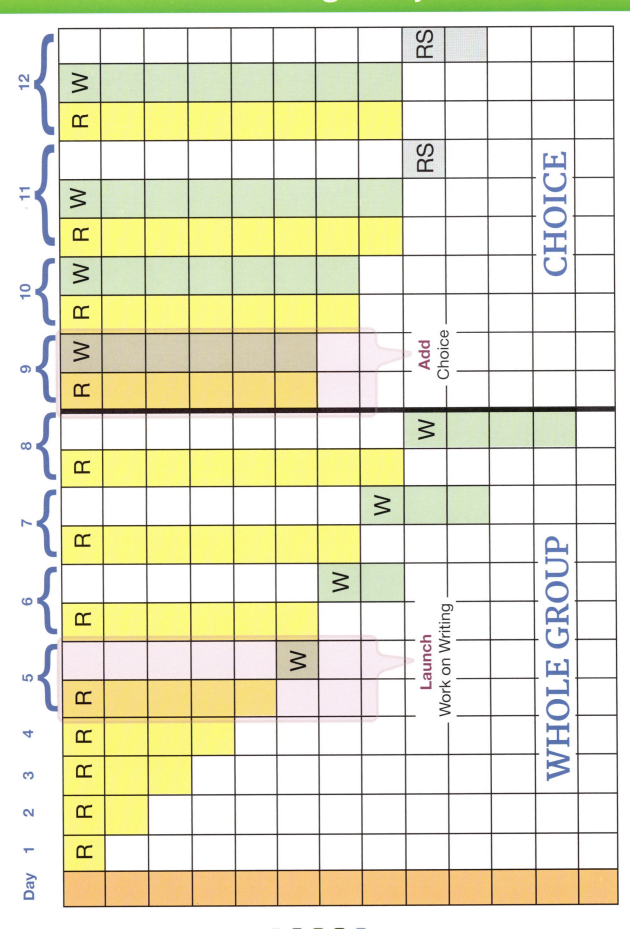

Keeping Track of Daily 5 Choices

Children love knowing what will happen during each day. Many teachers put daily schedules on their board and review it with their class each morning. Children refer to this throughout the day. Once it is on the board, children own the schedule and keep teachers on task. Very often you will hear, "Teacher, it's 10:30. We should be reading." There is comfort in knowing what to expect. As with any schedule, once children learn the structure and schedule of the Daily 5, they love it. Yet this schedule is different from the typical daily schedule in a few ways, both for the teacher and for the students.

One pronounced difference in the schedule for students is that they have choice regarding the order of participation in the Daily 5. Students will choose from five different tasks during the literacy block. When you enter a class that uses the Daily 5 as its literacy system, you see children Reading to Self, Reading to Someone, Listening to Reading, Working on Writing, and doing Word Work. These are all happening simultaneously. You will notice that each child has a strong sense of purpose, pride, and accomplishment. The order in which each child does these things can (and probably will) vary each day, according to how that child is feeling at the moment.

When teachers initially hear that children will have the power to choose what they will be doing during Daily 5, they may become nervous, since they have been used to owning the clock and the schedule along with owning the children's learning. This message to teachers, that they need to "own" their students' learning, can be found around every corner in education. Teachers are given textbooks and told to "teach this to your children." Teachers are given curriculum schedules that dictate, "You will teach this on this day."

However, when teachers trust students to make responsible choices, students gain control over their own learning. Children who are invited to decide the order of tasks, to choose their own partner, or to choose a strategy that works for them perceive themselves as more competent and more involved in their learning. Students who are given the opportunity to select appropriate cognitive or metacognitive strategies for comprehension will feel greater ownership of their achievement (Turner and Paris, 1995). However, at times the biggest challenge with choice is how to manage it.

Below is the form we use to help us manage and keep track of the choices our students make each day. We run off a number of them and keep them on a clipboard in our whole-group instruction area. Before each round of Daily 5, whether we do two, three, four, or five rounds, we have children "check in" verbally with us, and we record their choice on this chart with a coding system: R=Read to Self, RS=Read to Someone, W=Work on Writing, WW=Word Work, L=Listen to Reading.

Recording their choice on the sheet accomplishes a number of things. When students verbally check in and see us record their Daily 5 selection, it is like forming a contract for what they will do and helps them get started right away. This check-in also allows us to keep track of each student's choices so we can nudge them to vary their Daily 5 choice if necessary.

Daily 5 Check-In Form

Name												

R = Read to Self   **W** = Work on Writing   **RS** = Read to Someone   **WW** = Word Work   **L** = Listen to Reading

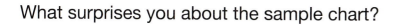

Review the Launching Daily 5 Foundation Lessons chart.

What surprises you about the sample chart?

How might you change the way you launch Daily 5 based on the charts?

How might you adjust or adapt the schedule in your classroom?

TRUST Choice R-E-S-P-E-C-T

Seat Work **Centers** **Workshop** **Daily 5**

BUSY WORK

LOW Trust & Respect
LOW Choice

Teacher's Time: Creating and Correcting Student Work

Student Achievement

HIGH Trust & Respect
HIGH Choice

Teacher's Time: Working with Students

READING & WRITING

What have you learned in the Daily 5 presentation that is pushing you out of a comfort zone?

What is most comfortable about Daily 5?

Where are you most in agreement with your grade-level teaching colleagues when it comes to literacy instruction?

What are the biggest differences in how your staff members teach reading and writing?

Literacy Block Schedule Sample

Primary

Weeks 6+ or after Daily 5 or Literacy Routines Are in Place

8:50–9:00	Day begins, gather on rug, take attendance, opening poem
9:00–9:15	CAFE Focus Lesson—Comprehension with a picture book
9:15–9:35	Round 1 of Daily 5—Teacher works with small group, then confers with 3–4 students
9:35–9:45	CAFE Focus Lesson—Accuracy
9:45–10:05	Round 2 of Daily 5—Teacher works with small group, then confers with 3–4 students
10:05–10:15	CAFE Focus Lesson—Fluency/Expand Vocabulary
10:15–10:35	Round 3 of Daily 5—Teacher works with small group, then confers with 3–4 students Share/Review of Strategies
10:35–10:45	Shared Writing/Writer's Workshop
10:45–11:25	Ready for lunch
11:25–11:30	Lunch and recess
11:30–12:10	Math Daily 5
12:10–1:30	Flex Block: PE/Music 2X per week, Social Studies,
1:30–2:30	Science, Research
2:30–2:50	Recess
2:50–3:20	Chapter book
3:20	Dismissal

Times are approximate and vary

Literacy Block Schedule Sample

Intermediate

Weeks 6+ or after Daily 5 or Literacy Routines Are in Place

8:50–9:00	Day begins, gather on rug, take attendance, opening poem
9:00–9:25	CAFE Focus Lesson—Comprehension with a picture book
9:25–10:10	Round 1 of Daily 5—Teacher works with small group, then confers with 5–8 students
10:10–10:35	Focus Lesson—Writing
10:35–11:15	Round 2 of Daily 5—Teacher works with small group, then confers with 5–8 students
11:15–11:30	Share/Review of Strategies
11:30–12:10	Lunch and recess
12:10–1:30	Math
1:30–2:30	Flex Block: PE/Music 2X per week, Social Studies, Science, Research
2:30–2:50	Recess
2:50–3:20	Chapter book
3:20	Dismissal

Times are approximate and vary

What can I do to support teachers who are implementing Daily 5 and CAFE?

● **Understand the Change Dynamic**

Understand the change model and have addressed all of the categories with my staff for a successful implementation

● **Research Base**

Have core knowledge of best practices

Have read The Daily 5 book, The CAFE Book, and have watched many videos

● **Differentiation**

Understand that each staff member's needs for support are different and have identified for myself and with them what is most supportive for their learning

● **Instruction**

I know that no one program will meet the needs of all students, and I encourage courageous conversations with my staff and district staff about how to support our students

● **Focus Lessons**

Support professional development with my staff on how instruction is tailored to student needs based on assessment information

I know the assessments and can interpret them

Teachers' focus lessons will be short, focused, and explicit

Encourage teachers to spend the most time teaching one-on-one, some time teaching small groups, and less time teaching whole group

Listen and observe students actively engaged in lessons through Listen and Talk

● **Student Choice**

Observe teachers teaching students how to build stamina using the 10 Steps to Independence

Students will be reading materials that are at their own levels

Watch to see that students have much choice over materials they read when in classrooms

Observe that teachers are giving students opportunities for lots of authentic reading and writing practice during each school day

● **Small Group**

Understand that using reading level isn't the primary determiner for placing students into a group; it is one determiner

Understand students will be grouped by skill and strategy needs with knowledge of reading level

Understand how to manage flexible groups through the use of the paper or electronic Pensieve, assessments, and progress monitoring

● **Conferring**

All adults working with children teach toward the same goal and strategy set by the teacher

Understand progress monitoring and how to use Touch Points

Listen in to see that students read from material at their own level when in classrooms

Realize that fair is not always equal. Students' needs determine how often we meet with them. Those of highest need will be met with more often than lowest-need students (see Richard Allington)

(continued)

What can I do to support teachers who are implementing Daily 5 and CAFE?

🟠 **Assessing and Evaluating**

We have a schoolwide plan for assessing students 3–4 times a year, reviewing data information, and collaborate on ways to support teachers and students to address the needs of all students

🟠 **Sharing and Celebrating**

Students and teachers will share their learning and celebrate their successes. Create systems to accomplish this

🟠 **Interactive Read-Aloud**

Each day teachers will be reading aloud and modeling CAFE strategies

🟠 **Robust Materials**

Create a budget using school and district funds for books that are at students' own level and interest

Ensure teachers and students have many books available to them in their classroom libraries, school library, and book rooms. If we have a basal program, I know that no one program will meet the needs of all students.

Courageous conversations are encouraged with my staff and district staff about how to support our students by using best practices

🟠 **Support Classroom Design**

Understand classroom design, how it supports successful implementation of the Daily 5 and the CAFE, and encourage teachers to make the classroom work as the second teacher in the class

Daily 5 and CAFE Leadership Support Survey

Please indicate areas where you would like support:

Daily 5
- ☐ Set up Read to Self, including support lessons
- ☐ Set up Work on Writing, including support lessons
- ☐ Set up Read to Someone, including support lessons
- ☐ Set up Word Work, including support lessons
- ☐ Set up Listen to Reading, including support lessons
- ☐ Barometer Child
- ☐ Planning Foundation Lessons

Student Choice
- ☐ Building Stamina
- ☐ Handing off Daily 5 choice to students
- ☐ Supporting student book choice
- ☐ Supporting student writing choice

Assessing
- ☐ Administering reading assessments
- ☐ Analyzing assessment data and setting student goals
- ☐ Setting up assessment materials and student assessment

Whole Group
- ☐ Develop Curriculum Calendar
- ☐ Using CAFE and Curriculum Calendar to design lessons
- ☐ Understanding interactive read-aloud, teaching skills and strategies

Focus Lessons
- ☐ Skill and strategy instruction
- ☐ Short and explicit
- ☐ Student engagement during instruction

Small Group
- ☐ Grouping students by skills and strategies
- ☐ Keeping the lesson short—what is the structure
- ☐ Record keeping and grading
- ☐ Resources in our school and beyond

Conferring
- ☐ Setting up conferring notebook
- ☐ Touch points and grading
- ☐ What is the structure, and what does it look like?
- ☐ Using the CAFE Menu to support decisions or strategy

Sharing and Celebrating
- ☐ Setting up the structure

Classroom Design
- ☐ Whole-group and small-group meeting area
- ☐ Classroom library
- ☐ Student work space
- ☐ Teacher area
- ☐ Setting up the CAFE Menu

Additional Thoughts:

Welcome!

Thanks so much for coming! This wonderful group of children responds very well to kind, positive words. They are very independent and know the routines well, so I'm sure your day will run smoothly. Don't hesitate to honor them by following their lead; they are a great group!

Schedule at a Glance

8:40–8:55	Students enter when they arrive at school (open campus) and begin book shopping
8:55	School starts: attendance, welcome, etc.
9:00–9:15	Calendar
9:15–11:50	Daily 5 and Writer's Workshop
11:50–12:50	Lunch and recess
12:50–2:00	Math
2:00–2:30	Third block (student-initiated time, Science/SS, Handwriting, Art)
2:30–2:50	Recess
2:50–3:20	Chapter book
3:20	Dismissal

Students Enter

Students will begin coming into the room about 8:40 or whenever they arrive at school. Please remind them to 1) order lunch 2) check in on the Daily Graph 3) grab their book boxes 4) read or shop for "good-fit books." They will do this until the bell rings at 8:55.

School Starts

Day begins: Ask helpers to count up lunches. You will record lunches and absent students on the attendance report, which is in the blue folder. Helpers will take this report to the office. The daily helpers will assist you throughout the day.

Review the schedule with students. Ask if they can make a true statement about the Daily Graph.

Stand and recite the flag salute, and then have the helpers lead the class over to the math calendar.

Calendar

The helpers will begin leading the calendar. You act as a participant as the helpers manage and run the calendar time.

Move into shared reading on the carpet: today's literature selection is Skippyjon Jones. We are working on modeling fluency as well as the strategy Back Up and Reread as a way to fix up Check for Understanding if and when comprehension breaks down or when a word is read incorrectly.

Daily 5

Here is the structure of Daily 5: Call each child's name, one by one, referring to the Daily 5 clipboard. On the clipboard, mark their choice in the next blank box using the coding system (R = Read to Self, RS = Read to Someone, W = Work on Writing, WW = Word Work, and L = Listen to Reading). Helpers will keep count for Read to Someone as we take a maximum of 8 people for Read to Someone per round. Once kids are done checking in, total how many Read to Someone kids there are. It must be even or someone will have to make a change. Dismiss them in the following order: Listen to Reading first, then Read to Self, followed by Work on Writing, Word Work, and finally the children doing Read to Someone. Since only Read to Someone students are left, they will easily be able to find a partner and head out. Dismissing in this manner allows for a calmer start so there is not a mad rush.

At this time I usually pull a small focused reading or writing group and do one-on-one conferences. Today, rather than pull any small groups, please move around the room reading with kids, helping with their writing, etc. On my desk, you will find my brown polka-dot conferring notebook. You can use the notebook to guide you as you work with children. Inside is a tabbed section for each child. It will tell you what their goals are in reading and writing, as well as the teaching strategy I have been using to guide their instruction. As you meet with children, their conferring page in the notebook can help guide your conversation with them. Feel free to jot a note on their conferring page. Your input is valued.

Please spend some time with the students in the Word Work area. We are working with the little ones on letter formation and learning their sight words.

Please make it a priority to spend 2–4 minutes with the following students during Daily 5: Jesse, Mariah, Micah, and Treven. You will see what we are working on based on their conferring sheet. Read with other students as time permits.

After about 20–25 minutes, or when kids are showing signs of losing their stamina and focus, ring the chimes (on the square shelves to the left of my desk). Call the kids back up to the green carpet. I usually do a focus lesson here. However, since you are a guest, please have 3 or 4 students model for the class their reading strategy this week or share a writing strategy as the focus lesson.

Then using the clipboard, repeat the above procedure, having students make a choice for round 2. They must make a new choice. Dismiss the group as detailed above. You'll rotate through the class again, working with different children.

After about 20–25 minutes or when their stamina is waning, ring chimes again, pulling them back to the rug, and read through the poems behind the little brown chair by the chart rack. See if the students can locate the new sight words, which are on the white board in the gathering space.

Using the clipboard, have kids check in for round 3, indicating their choice in the next column. They will make a choice that is different from their first two. Dismiss the group as detailed above. Again, you will rotate through the group working with individuals. Signal with the chimes after about 20 minutes, inviting them back up to the gathering spot.

We end the morning with a share time. Some may want to share writing and some a strategy or a piece of reading.

The children are so well trained that not only can they tell you how to do Daily 5, but they probably WILL tell you how, especially if you veer in any way from their well-internalized routine. If you have any questions, don't hesitate to ask any of the students in the room.

Writer's Workshop

The lesson in the Lucy Calkins book is marked. You will want to preview it before you begin. The lesson should take no more than 10 minutes and then students will proceed to independent writing time. Please use the conferring notebook to guide your conferences with individuals. Come together and allow for a brief time of sharing before preparing for lunch.

11:47—Ready for lunch

Dear Parents and Guardians,

Welcome to a new school year! I hope you had a wonderful summer and enjoyed spending quality time with your child. I know that each year of your child's schooling presents new expectations and routines for you and your child to become familiar with. I will be introducing classroom routines and structure in a way that removes all of the guesswork from the child and allows them to concentrate fully on learning. In reading, the classroom structure I use is called Daily 5. Soon your child will be talking about "the Daily 5" at home. The purpose of this letter is to explain to you what the Daily 5 is and what you should expect to see at home.

The Daily 5 is a literacy structure that teaches independence and gives children the skills needed to create a lifetime love of reading and writing. It consists of five tasks that are introduced individually. When introduced to each task, the children discuss what it looks like, sounds like, and feels like to engage in the task independently. Then, the children work on building their stamina until they are successful at being independent while doing that task.

These are the five tasks:
- Read to Self
- Work on Writing
- Read to Someone
- Listen to Reading
- Word Work

When all five tasks have been introduced and the children are fully engaged in reading and writing, I am able to work with small groups and confer with children one-on-one. This structure is effective, the results are amazing, and the children look forward to Daily 5 time.

One thing you may notice is a decrease in the number of worksheets your child brings home. Although worksheets keep students busy, they don't result in the high level of learning we want for your child.

Ask your child about Daily 5 and Math Daily 3 and see what they have to say. I anticipate your child will tell you about the class stamina, how we are working towards independence, and maybe you will even hear about some of the fantastic things your child has written, read, or listened to during our Daily 5 time. Please feel free to contact me with any questions you may have.

Thank you for your continued support!

When creating a culture for learning and independence, two essential components must be in place . . . a gathering place and focus lessons.

A gathering place is an open space large enough for the whole class to gather while sitting on the floor. The space also includes a chart rack and whiteboard for focus lessons, class-created anchor (or living) charts, an overhead projector or document camera, a CAFE Menu board, and other teaching materials. We have a gathering place in every classroom in which we teach, regardless of our students' age level.

Behavior management through proximity and an elimination of the convenient distractions that desks hold are two of the biggest payoffs of a gathering space. Sitting in a group provides students with an opportunity to turn and talk, enhancing engagement, and giving each one an opportunity to express their thinking. In addition, being able to move from their independent work space to the gathering place provides a needed brain and body break. There is a general rule of direct instruction: the approximate number of years our children are in age is the approximate number of minutes their brains are able to be engaged and processing information when we deliver direct instruction. Keeping our whole-group focus lessons shorter and to the point results in better retention of the concepts we are trying to teach.

We know that children can build their stamina, eventually maintaining independence for 30–45 minutes, but asking children to sustain for longer than they are able results in off-task behavior and lower levels of performance. We signal children to the gathering place between Daily 5 rounds. This accomplishes two things at once: it provides time for a shift in their brainwork and offers much needed movement of their bodies (which is why some people call it a brain and body break). As children come to join us in the gathering place on the floor, it signals the shift in activity and thinking, from whatever Daily 5 choice they were just participating in to a focus lesson.

Students come to expect that in between each round of Daily 5, they will not only have some much needed time of movement for their bodies, but will also receive short bursts of valuable and focused instruction. It is this consistent pattern that leads to the lovely ebb and flow of teaching and practicing, teaching and practicing, that exemplifies the Daily 5.

Allington, Richard. 2009. *What Really Matters in Response to Intervention: Research-Based Designs*. Boston, MA: Pearson Education.

----------. 2012. *What Really Matters for Struggling Readers: Designing Research-Based Programs*. Boston, MA: Pearson Education.

Allington, Richard, and Peter Johnston. 2002. *Reading to Learn: Lessons From Exemplary Fourth-Grade Classrooms*. New York: Guilford Press.

Anderson, R.C., P. T. Wilson, and L. C. Fielding. 1988. "Growth in Reading and How Children Spend Their Time Outside of School." Reading Research Quarterly, 23, 285—303.

Atwell, Nancie. 1987. *In the Middle: Writing, Reading, and Learning with Adolescents*. Portsmouth, NH: Heinemann.

Beck, Isabel, Margaret McKeown and Linda Kucan. 2013. *Bringing Words to Life: Robust Vocabulary Instruction*. New York: Guilford Press.

----------. 1946. *Foundations of Reading Instruction*. New York: American Book Co.

Betts, Emmett. 1949. "Adjusting Instruction to Individual Needs." In The Forth-Eighth Yearbook of the National Society for the Study of Education: Part II, Reading in the School, ed. N. B. Henry. Chicago: University of Chicago Press.

Boushey Gail, and Joan Moser. 2009. *The CAFE Book: Engaging All Students in Daily Literacy Assessment and Instruction*. Portland, ME: Stenhouse.

----------. 2009. The Daily CAFE. http://www.thedailycafe.com.

----------. 2012. CAFE Conferring Pensieve. http://www.ccpensieve.com.

----------. 2014. *The Daily Five: Fostering Literacy Independence in the Elementary Grades*. Second Edition. Portland, ME: Stenhouse.

Buckner, Aimee. 2005. *Notebook Know-How: Strategies for the Writer's Notebook*. Portland, ME: Stenhouse.

Calkins, Lucy, Mary Ehrenworth, and Christopher Lehman. 2012. *Pathways to the Common Core: Accelerating Achievement*. Portsmouth, NH: Heinemann.

Coulton, Mia. 2001. *Look at Danny*. Beachwood, OH: Mary Ruth Books.

Farstrup, A. E., and S. J. Samuels, eds. 2011. *What Research Has to Say About Reading Instruction*. 4th ed. Newark, DE: International Reading Association.

Fisher, Douglas, Nancy Frey, and Diane Lapp. 2009. *In a Reading State of Mind: Brain Research, Teacher Modeling, and Comprehension Instruction*. Newark, DE: International Reading Association.

Fletcher, Ralph, and JoAnn Portalupi. 2013, 1993. *What a Writer Needs*. Portland, ME: Stenhouse.

Fisher, Douglas, Nancy Frey, and Diane Lapp. 2009. *In a Reading State of Mind: Brain Research, Teacher Modeling, and Comprehension Instruction*. Newark, DE: International Reading Association.

Gallagher, Kelly. 2009. *Readicide: How Schools Are Killing Reading and What You Can Do About It*. Portland, ME: Stenhouse.

----------. 2011. *Write Like This: Teaching Real-World Writing Through Modeling & Mentor Texts*. Portland, ME: Stenhouse.

Gambrell, L.B., R.M. Wilson, and W.N. Gantt. 1981. "Classroom Observations of Task-Attending Behaviors of Good and Poor Readers." Journal of Educational Research 74(6): 400–404.

(continued)

Gambrell, Linda. 2011. "Seven Rules of Engagement: What's Most Important to Know about Motivation to Read." The Reading Teacher 65.3, 172—178.

Grinder, Michael. 1995. *ENVoY: Your Personal Guide to Classroom Management*. Battle Ground, WA: Michael Grinder and Associates.

Hattie, John. 2008. *Visible Learning: A Synthesis of Over 800 Meta-Analyses Relating to Achievement*. New York, NY: Routledge.

----------. 2012. *Visible Learning for Teachers: Maximizing Impact on Learning*. New York, NY: Routledge.

Howard, Mary. 2009. *RTI from All Sides: What Every Teacher Needs to Know*. Portsmouth, NH: Heinemann.

----------. 2012. *Good to Great Teaching: Focusing on the Literacy Work That Matters*. Portsmouth, NH: Heinemann.

Krashen, Stephen. 2004. *The Power of Reading: Insights from the Research*. Portsmouth, NH: Heinemann.

Marten, Cindy. 2003. *Word Crafting: Teaching Spelling, Grades K–6*. Portsmouth, NH: Heinemann.

Medina, John. 2009. *Brain Rules: 12 Principles for Surviving and Thriving at Work, Home and School*. Seattle, WA: Pear Press.

Miller, Debbie. 2002. *Reading with Meaning: Teaching Comprehension in the Primary Grades*. Portland, ME: Stenhouse.

Miller, Donalyn. 2009. *The Book Whisperer: Awakening the Inner Reader in Every Child*. San Francisco, CA: Jossey-Bass.

Mooney, Margaret. 1990. *Reading To, With and By Children*. Katonah, NY: Richard C. Owen.

Morrow, Lesley Mandel, Linda Gambrell, and Michael Pressley. 2007. *Best Practices in Literacy Instruction*. New York: Guilford Press.

Pressley, Michael, Richard Allington, Ruth Wharton-McDonald, Cathy Collins Block, and Lesley Mandel Morrow. 2001. *Learning to Read: Lessons from Exemplary First-Grade Classrooms*. New York: Guilford Press.

Ray, Katie Wood. 2010. *In Pictures and In Words: Teaching the Qualities of Good Writing Through Illustration Study*. Portsmouth, NH: Heinemann.

Routman, Regie. 2003. *Reading Essentials: The Specifics You Need to Teach Reading Well*. Portsmouth, NH: Heinemann.

----------. 2005. *Writing Essentials: Raising Expectations and Results While Simplifying Teaching*. Portsmouth, NH: Heinemann.

Samuels, S. Jay, and Alan E. Farstrup, eds. 2011. *What Research Has to Say About Reading Instruction*. 4th ed. Newark, DE: International Reading Association.

Scientific Learning Corporation. 2008. "Adding Ten Minutes of Reading Time Dramatically Changes Levels of Print Exposure. Educator's Briefing. http://www.iowaafterschoolalliance.org/documents/cms/docs/10_minutes.pdf.

Tough, Paul. 2012. *How Children Succeed: Grit, Curiosity, and the Hidden Power of Character*. New York, NY: Houghton Mifflin Harcourt.

Wesson, Ken. 2001. "A Conversation about Learning and the Brain-compatible Classroom" hosted by Susan Kovalik and Associates, Federal Way, Washington, January 12, 2001.

UPPER IOWA UNIVERSITY
Established in 1857®

Earn 1 Graduate Level Professional Development Credit
Participating in an Educational Design Live Workshop

Course Description

Live workshop / Online Seminar: This course offers educators the opportunity to earn one credit for each workshop or seminar attended. A research reflection paper is required for the Daily 5 workshop/seminar, and a separate research reflection paper is required for the CAFE workshop/ seminar.

Credit Information

Upon successful completion of an approved workshop and the accompanying requirements, Upper Iowa University will award one semester hour of graduate level professional development credit. These credits are predominantly used for professional advancement (increase on pay scale or recertification), and are not part of a degree program. It is the student's responsibility to verify approval from appropriate district or college officials before attempting to use these credits to satisfy any degree, state recertification, or school district requirements. Upper Iowa will not assume responsibility if a credit is not accepted due to the location of the university or criteria of credit acceptance. State licensing departments, school districts, and other degree programs vary regarding their criteria for credit acceptance. Clock Hours - Many states accept regionally accredited two- or four-year college credit at the 100 (freshman) level or above to be used toward maintenance. One semester hour of college credit is the equivalent of 15 clock hours. State licensing departments and school districts vary regarding their criteria for credit acceptance. It is your responsibility to check with your individual state or district.

Course Requirements

For each credit:

1. Attend a 2 Sisters Workshop.

2. Once you have completed the workshop, complete the appropriate "Getting Started" guide for your workshop. (If you attend both workshops you will need to complete both "Getting Started" guides. They can be found at http://www.thedailycafe.com/public/2381.cfm. Reflect on your learning and the impact it will have on you in your current position in education. What research was highlighted and what implications does it have for you as a professional? Adhering to the guidelines below, write a 2-3 page reflective essay (one for each workshop attended) about your learning.

> Research Reflection Paper Guidelines
> ☒ Paper must include a Title Page with your name, address, title of course and course number, workshop or seminar completion date and date sent.
> ☒ Use a 12 point font and one inch margins. Staple the paper together. Do not use a report cover.
> ☒ Your reflective research paper should include highlights of your learning about Daily 5 and CAFE. What do you agree with? What challenges do you face? What research reinforces the philosophy of Daily 5/ CAFE?
> ☒ You must reference a minimum of 3 sources, using correct APA format for in-text citations and the bibliography.
> ☒ This paper is an individual assignment to be completed by the individual receiving the credit. Group papers will not be accepted.

You will be graded on the accuracy of the previous guidelines, and according to the attached rubric.

3. Send in your Educational Design completion certificate, along with the Upper Iowa University registration form, payment, and your research reflection paper.   Grades will be entered following UIU's 6 term schedule. Please allow 6 – 8 weeks for grading.

Submitting Report

• A copy of your online course completion participation certificate must be included with your report to be accepted for grading.

• Your registration and paper are due (postmarked) six months from the end date of the workshop. Extensions are not allowed. Your paper will not be returned to you. Grades will be determined according to the rubric. Allow 6 – 8 weeks for grading. Transcripts may be requested following the link below.

If you wish to receive feedback, include a self-addressed, postage paid envelope with your registration materials.

Transcripts

Transcripts are available at www.getmytranscript.org eight weeks after your materials are received.

Checklist to Register for Graduate Credit

To earn credit complete the following:

Please _**initial**_ next to each line and _**sign**_ at the bottom to indicate completion.

_____ I have included my Educational Design workshop completion certificate.

_____ I have included my Upper Iowa University Registration Form and this completed checklist.

_____ I have included payment **(check or credit card information)**.

_____ I have included a 2-3 page research reflection paper (including references and adhering to APA guidelines) for each workshop I wish to receive credit. (If I attended both CAFE and Daily 5, I have a paper for each.)

_____ I have viewed the grading rubric and have followed required guidelines to receive credit.

_____ All of my materials are included in one envelope and are being sent together.

_____ I understand that if I **wish to receive feedback**, I must include a self-addressed, postage paid envelope along with registration materials. UIU will not be responsible for lost or damaged items.

_____ All materials are being submitted within six months of completing the workshop or seminar.

_____ I understand that it will require up to 8 weeks for processing and grading, and I am responsible for requesting my transcripts after the 8 week period.

_____ I understand that the above criteria must be completed to receive credit. **Due to high volume, incomplete packets will not be processed or returned.**

_____   _____
Signature   Date

Mail this completed form along with the above materials to:

Upper Iowa University Mesa Center
Daily 5/CAFE Workshop Credit
1361 S. Alma School Rd.
Mesa, AZ 85210

For further questions, email: dailyfive@uiu.edu

Grading Rubric

Name:	Course Title (As listed on registration form):
Address:	Grader:
Date:	Total Points: _____ Grade A B C F

Requirements

Qualities & Criteria	Exceeds Expectations (4)	Meets Expectations (3)	Needs Improvement (0-2)
Explanation of Topic 4 pts. _____	Writer introduces topic and clearly identifies relevance to his/her classroom.	Writer makes reader aware of topic.	No reference to topic or problem.
Content (2X) 8 pts. _____	Workshop content is covered in depth; incorporates current research; Application to classroom is specific and insights and challenges are identified and elaborated upon .	Content is adequately covered but not in depth and research is referenced. Insights and challenges are noted but not explored thoroughly.	Content is limited, repetitive or quoted excessively. Little or no reference to current research. Discussion of insights and challenges was limited or missing.
Clarity & Correctness of Writing (.5X) 2 pts. _____	Writing is clear and concise with no errors in spelling and grammar.	Few errors in spelling and grammar and they do not cause confusion in content; generally clear writing.	Contains multiple spelling & grammatical errors; writing lacks clarity
Conclusions 4 pts. _____	Writer synthesizes strategies and research and connects them with classroom practice. Succinct and precise conclusions based on the review of the literature.	Writer provides concluding remarks with an analysis & synthesis of information; some conclusions not fully supported.	Limited effort or success at synthesizing research and practice.
Sources & Citations (.5X) 2 pts. _____	APA styles is used throughout and all citations and references are accurate .	APA style is used inconsistently or there are minor issues with accuracy of citations.	APA style is not followed. Works cited in text are not consistent with reference list.

Grade Scale: A = 20-18, B = 17 – 16, C = 15 – 14, F = 13 - Lower

One test of the correctness of educational procedure is the happiness of the child.

—Maria Montessori

The most basic and powerful way to connect to another person is to listen. Just listen. Perhaps the most important thing we ever give each other is our attention. A loving silence often has far more power to heal and to connect than the most well-intentioned words.

—Rachel Naomi Remen

After you've done a thing the same way for two years, look it over carefully. After five years, look at it with suspicion. And after ten years, throw it away and start all over.

—Alfred Edward Pearlman

Notes

If you want to truly
understand something, try
to change it.

—Kurt Lewin

Success and failure are both greatly overrated. But failure gives you a whole lot more to talk about.
— Hildegard Knef

Spoon feeding, in the long
run teaches us nothing but
the shape of the spoon.
—E.M. Forster

Teaching reading IS rocket science.

—Louisa Moats

As the child approaches a new text he is entitled to an introduction so that when he reads, the gist of the story can provide some guide for a fluent reading.

—Marie Clay

Notes

The pleasure of all reading
is doubled when one lives
with another who shares
the same books.
—Katherine Mansfield

Notes

The libraries have become
my candy store.
—Juliana Kimball

A desk is a dangerous place from which to view the world.

—John Le Carre

Obstacles are those
frightful things you see
when you take your eyes
off the goal.

—Henry Ford

Notes

Acceptance of prevailing standards often means we have no standards of our own.

—Jean Toomer

If you are a struggling reader, all you have to do is look tough and say nothing, and then you will become invisible.

—Richard Vacca

Nobody can go back and
start a new beginning, but
anyone can start today
and make a new ending.
　　　—Maria Robinson

Notes

True genius resides in the capacity for evaluation of uncertain, hazardous, and conflicting information.
—Winston Churchill

The doors we open and
close each day decide
the lives we live.
—Flora Whittemore

The teachers I work with continue to assess our thinking on assessment. One question that guides our conversation is "Who will learn something if we do this?"
—Joanne Hindley Salch

It takes a lot of courage to release the familiar and seemingly secure, to embrace the new. But there is no real security in what is no longer meaningful. There is more security in the adventurous and exciting, for in movement there is life, and in change there is power.

—Alan Cohen

Even when freshly washed and relieved of all obvious confections, children tend to be sticky.

—Fran Lebowitz

What is our praise or pride
but to imagine excellence
and try to make it.
—Richard Wilbur

"It's our choices, Harry, that show what we truly are, far more than our abilities."

—J.K. Rowling

A book is like a garden carried in the pocket.
—Chinese Proverb

Notes

When we reflect on why things work for a few students, we can begin to formulate a stance toward all students, a stance based on our commitment to respect the depth of their potential and the dignity of their person.

—Robert Fried